Racing Toward the Sun

Joshua Gulliford

ISBN: 9798451175958

Where My Mother Lives

This is peace,

This is zin,

This is where my mother lives.

Collecting hope,

Drowning in passion,

Bathing in sun like fresh roses

Thorns that protect her soul,

Giving her strength,

Silence her fear,

She's secure.

This is where my mother lives,

Warm, illuminated, embraced,

Content with all emotion,

Blessed…Blessed

This is where my mother lives

In kingdom,

In roots,

seeping out like hickory tree sap,

Blowing,

Flowing through her river streams,

Like warm milk.

This is where my mother lives

Surviving, defeating, conquering

Rebelling with ease,

Relieving her spirit,

Reviving her heart

This is where my mother lives

She lives in my worries,

She lives in my wounds,

She lives in my visions,

She lives in my moments,

She lives in my desires

She lives in my faith,

She lives in my love,

She loved...She loves.

She is love,

That is where my mother lives.

My Children

I will jump off ten cliffs

If it saves your life

I will walk a thousand miles

If it let you fly

I would rush around the world

So you can take your time

I'll do anything for you

I will swim across the ocean

If that makes you smile

I will love you to forever

It might take a while.

I will take away your pain

And leave it to drown

I'll do anything for you

I will teach you to be lion

So, you can roar

I will sacrifice my dreams

If it makes you soar

I will take a little less

So, you can have more

I'll do anything for you

I will walk on burning coals

If it keeps you warm

I will hold your umbrella

When it starts to storm

I will take away your sorrow

So, you don't have to mourn

I'll do anything for you

Happiness

I sing more than one hymn

Hold a note for free

I salsa to more than one beat

And swim through like breeze.

I shout love from mountain tops

That were designed to fall

Gathering redemption as wisdom

Instead of losing it all.

I bring faith to what was burn in the fire,

I heal what was cut down by wire.

I am no secret, I make no sense, I'm in your spirit.

I speak as your communication to embrace.

A broke creation,

that tumbles to one side when alone.

I am your freedom, I am your result, I am your home.

I give you deeper breaths than the ocean waves,

I praise in what was given

And less in what was gave.

When everything is torn

I am your slave.

I spread easy as sand

And run for miles.

And when you least expect it

I am your smile.

I place dreams in ones who realize

A redwood can grow from a seed

I am more than just myself,

I am me.

I am what makes you possible

I release, I'm determine, and I am unstoppable

I take place of what was stole from you

And knock it down to be slain

I wipe your tears that pour down like the rain

And as everything washes away

So does your pain.

Take It

Take these seemingly empty hands

Grab this, have it

It completely belongs to you

So here take it

I love you

Love you like oxygen

Like a poor man love a smile

I love you

Like a kite love the breeze

I love you, like I love me

I love you

I love you sad like the blues

Love you deeper

Harder

Wider

Closer

Rougher

Stronger

I love you

No friend, no mom, no dad, no sibling

I love you like God loves you

I can do that

So here...

Take these seemly empty hands

It's yours...

My heart...

Take it

It belongs to you.

Say Her Name...

Buried alive

she rather be buried alive

Then ever feel their skin

Their murky russet skin

Slinking from behind her

The pressure swallowed into her back

Hammering her down to the asphalt

Their skin, their cold blood skin

produced welts on her face

Before tearing apart her temple of armor

Their skin divulged, as she scraps the concrete

Blooding fingers are not worth their skin

Clutching her down

Their skin thick like butcher knifes

Carving into her veins

Like sandpaper

Puncturing, destroying, obliterating

Her sanctuary

her haven

her refuge

In and out, In an out, in an out

Each piece of skin like lifeless meat

Took its turn splitting her God bestowed vessel in thirds

The skin left their mark on her thighs

Like black oil smoldering in her pours

Then with a laugh they stripped the skin from her bones

And left their fingerprint on her soul.

That One Gay Boy

Weaken rainbow remember your name

Shine like strength, the purpose is to gain.

Pull the shaded cloud from over your head

Arise from your tears, if it is heard, it was said.

Stand up against the circumstance

Show your shades at glance

Polish you're glow

Then recognize your colors are beautiful

Weaken rainbow remember your name.

Dirty

I'm dirty, after all that time

I scrubbed and I wiped but you

You walked all over me.

Wiped your nasty shoes on my heart,

Now I'm dirty.

You tip toed around my mind

And made me think that you were sanitary

But your filthy toes spread across my lips

Down to my ankles

And I am dirty.

You went away to play in the mud

Making your little mud pies

Thinking you could come home us my doormat

To wipe clean.

Because of you I'm dirty

You stomped dust on me, my pride, and my dignity

With the trifling stinky leftover trash

You made me dirty.

Kicked your feet up to relax,

like they weren't dripping from the rain.

An I should have let you stay out there a little longer

Because maybe you would come back washed and unsoiled

But you came home dirty

You made me dirty

And now my tears are all I have to make me clean again.

Racing Toward the Sun

I want to run

I want to run away from anybody who doubts us

I want to run from every moment that I didn't get to spend with you

I want to leave out all the hatred in those nights

Where love has walked out the door

And anger has introduced itself

I don't think you understand

I want my heart to love you more than me

I want us to redefine what making love means

I want to hold you every night until I've defeated your demons

And when the morning comes

I want to celebrate the fact that I got to watch

Your eyes open another day

I want us to forget the day we met...

I want to forget the day we met

So, we can reintroduce ourselves everyday

So everyday can be our anniversary

I want to look at you loving me look at you loving me

I want to act like were high school students

And I'll write you love notes

I want to purposely bump into each other knocking the box out your hand

And help you pick them up

And instead of skipping class

I will skip work and go broke just to be together

I want to run

I want to run as far as hope can take us

And when we come to that edge

And for a moment everything stops…

I want to jump

And while we're waiting for the gun to sound

I'll let you get a head start

But I won't let you get to far because I can't stand when we're apart

I want to love you as much as God loves you

Together we will win first place

And I'll let you hold the trophy

Can we run this blind race?

On your mark, get set,

Love me.

Laundry Day

I saw you in the store!

I liked you.

So, I tried you on,

And I loved you.

Then slowly your knitting came undone,

Your colors began to fade,

And unlike the rest of my closet

You held stains.

So, I took you off.

And I washed you.

Knitted you up and

Then dried out all the past,

And you shuck.

So, I folded you.

And placed you in my bottom drawer,

And I act as is you're not even there anymore.

Resentment

Dark lonely shapeless shadows

from shattered transparent seeping windows

on hallways of blank echoes blowing

through cold midnight secrets with rooms of dry air.

That's your love.

How hard does the needle have to poke?

In order for my love to leak out

In to a glass that is half empty

But wish to be half full.

You did everything but love me.

Morning Coffee

I felt the warmth

From your mug as I grace my figures around your

Warm smooth exterior,

As it eases me awake

And you hypnotize me with steam cleansing my face

Slowly pressing your stimulating hard glass

to my lips

they quiver, numb, and damp

It reminds me of succulent caramel

Fueling my tongue

Sending a soothing sensation

Through my body

And after the last drop

I set you back on your pedestal

And look deep into the bottom of the mug

And say "Good Morning".

Paralyzed

I stood there

Looking at you

I attempted not to smile

Out of habit

I clutched my arm so I couldn't wave

I enhanced my pace to get away

As I stand here, alone

And watch you walk away with him...

Evicted

Dead

Lazy, manipulative, abuse

You are dead

Bitter, frustration, attitude

You are dead,

Lies, deception, depression

You are dead

Anger, spiteful, deferred

Go to your room

You are dead

Cold, damaged, shattered

Close your coffin

You are now dead

And I will not be attending your funeral

You have lived in me for too long.

R.I.P.

Home

Where the road ends

And colors begin to fade

Where the secret lays

To the sun raise each day

Where the tea bag bathe

And my faith is saved

When the wind doesn't blow

And my peace is always known

Where sorrow never shows

And there is still hope

When the door doesn't close

And my feet aren't cold

You'll find me

My Name Is Lonely

My name is lonely

It's nice to meet you

I only sit in the corner of the room

hoping no one will notice me.

Eyes somehow see through every bit of my existence

But that's okay

I walk down the street with my head hung down

And no one pays attention.

I crawl through the depths of the world

Crying over...

Well...

Nobody

Because I am nobody

I got my name from heartache and pain

And I am related to tears.

My name is lonely

I sweep the floor when everyone is in the room

Only nobody stops to pick me up

I run into the arms of mental break downs for a reason

It's the only thing that invites me in.

My name is lonely

I climb to top of the mountains where people find peace

Reaching for the

Well, nothing I guess

I play the game of hide and seek

You hide I'll count

1, 2...3

No one hears me say the game is over

My name is lonely

I promise I will not bite

My hands may be shaking from being out in the cold

Feet may be swollen because no one wants to pick up a hitchhiker like me

My name is lonely

Can you see me

I've knocked on every door of every house

But their all to crowed for me

May I should just sit right here and close my eyes

Can you see me now?

Well maybe you can hear me!

I scream at the top of my lungs on to find

Everyone must have ear plugs

Cause after my voice is gone, I'm still alone

My damn name is lonely

Can you hear me now?

I realize I'm not perfect

But I'm working on my issues

Would you look at me if I look more like you, you, or you

Your disrespect is not taking lightly

So, here's what I need you to do

Let me reintroduce myself

My name is lonely

Now tell me

Who are you?

Black Man

Running fast in no directions

Swimming long but lost at sea

I'm on this earth but not for free

My ancestors are my humanity

Their dreams are my fantasy

Their love feels like a memory

Their pain is my destiny

So, until then...

I'll be mad at the world...

Until the worlds done being made at me.

Mirror Mirror On the Wall

See you,

Like you,

Hold you,

Kiss you,

Trust you,

Believe you,

Confide in you,

Protect you,

Search in you,

Find you,

Love me.

To My-In-Law

You should walk from other side of the room

Then introduce yourself to her, meet her

You should buy her one drink and complement her smile

She, you

But you don't ask for her number, not yet

Because what is meant to be will always be.

So, one day you see her in a coffee shop

You will both smile, familiar faces

You will sit there and talk at the corner table with her

Then you will walk

Now you can ask for her number

You'll make plans to pick her up Saturday at 7:15pm

But you she won't know you showed up at 6:59.

You can give her flowers and hug

A hug.

After time past…

Time past…

Time past…

You ask her dad

You will be allowed to propose

On a romantic evening

Will you... Yes

Then you will build a life with her

Protect, respect, intellect

You will manage the home

No too much, not too little

Just beautiful, just like her

You will be a great Father... Father, F-A-T-H-E-R

Like her father

She will be a loving mother

You will honor her

You will give her hope

You will give her a dream

You will give her love

Because her brother told her she desires it.

Faggot

They call me faggot

They label me sissy

They consider me weak

Because I choose to repeat

What I found I like.

So why do you care if I'm not your type?

I might bite the disrespect will make me want to fight

But I don't

Because they call me faggot

They label me sissy

The consider me weak

They beat me

Slung me, silenced my voice

And betongued me,

And refuse to hear me say

Call me by my name.

They remain playing these games

Immediately getting disgusted when I walk there way

Roll eyes, turn cheeks,

When I'm not the reason you are so damn unhappy.

Then they give me these rules to play by

And think I would just say okay, why?

Would I, be fine

With point end of the less than symbol

Pointed at me.

Why would I agree

To have you remind me

Who you think I should be?

I think it's crazy how

They call me faggot

They label me sissy

and they consider me weak.

They never even met me

They regret me

Before I have a chance to say hello

Before I can explain or share what I know.

Do I have mug me written on my forehead?

Do I have shoot me to place me in my death bed?

I get so fed up with it

Irritated as hell by it

But stay motivated from all this shit.

But

They still call me faggot

They label me sissy

And consider me weak

Well open your ears

While I explain somethings

Before some more ignorant shit out your mouth leaks

I am Joshua

J-O-S-H-U-A

Gay yes, scared no

Honest as hell, loyal for real

Prepared so beware

I'm content with who I am

And what I am

So, call me faggot

Label me sissy

Consider me weak

And all you will get from me is a smile

What reason do I have to speak?

You don't know me.

My Superwoman

My superwoman can't fly

Or make herself invisible

She can't pick up builds or throw cars

But my superwoman loves me

And not just any kind of love

The love from mother to son that lets you know

I'll protect you and you'll protect me.

But my superwoman is sick

Not sick with weakness but sick from pain

And I have watched as her opponent takes over,

As it defeats her slowly destroying everything, I knew was invincible

See if my superwoman

Could breathe take a deep breath and breathe out all her pain

She wouldn't even have to go through the stress of breathing

Because I'd do it for her.

I want my superwoman

I need my superwoman

I love my superwoman

So, I'd breathe out the stress of her saving the day

I'd breathe and erase all the wounds and scars from her battle

I'd breathe and blow out all her troubles.

And then

She would walk without hesitation

Then she could take a moment of hear the buzzing of bees

And the songs of birds.

She could spare a second to smell a field of roses

And she would dance with being bond to her restraints

But my superwoman does need all that

Because she is stronger than most

That's why she's super

She can fly and fall a hundred times a day

And still stand up again.

She could be defeated and bruised be tired and hungry

But still be glad woke her up this morning

My love for this superwoman is like a drug

Only I'm forever addicted

It like breathing I do it without notice

I wish I could save her like she saved me

And give her a break from breathing

Then she would realize how much the S on her chest

Means to Me.

Refund

Can I get a refund?

There was no warranty included in my purchase

Only a guarantee that you would expire on an arranged date

You were shiny and new in the beginning

But the new paint job wasn't thick enough to hide your scratches

I turn your ass in and collect the reward if I could

Like finding a lost dog.

The side effects were strong enough for me to pour you down the sink

I thought it was world

But it was only numbers on your stall

I built a wall…Slut

Can I get a refund please?

I kept my recites

Scars on my neck and back from the attempt at repairs proves it

Your customer service was good

But your community service was even better

Equal to your two-star rating all the door knob that you laid with

Hell, everyone but me had a key

You're a like a lost cell reception and your plan is cheap

But you can use this middle finger as my recite

Racing Toward the Sun

Made in the USA
Columbia, SC
16 August 2022

64752989R00022